This Book Belongs to:

...ERTON PRIMARY SCHOOL

Consultant: Fiona Moss RE Adviser, RE Today Services
Editor: Cathy Jones
Designer: Chris Fraser

Copyright © QED Publishing 2012

First published in the UK in 2012 by
QED Publishing
A Quarto Group company
230 City Road
London EC1V 2TT

www.qed-publishing.co.uk

A catalogue record for this book is available from the
British Library.

ISBN 978 1 84835 894 2

Printed in China

# Daniel
## •and the
# Lions

Written by Katherine Sully
Illustrated by Simona Sanfilippo

QED Publishing

Daniel was an important man. He was one of three ministers chosen by the king to help him rule the land.

Daniel worked hard. He soon became the king's favourite.

One day, the king decided to put Daniel in charge of everyone.

The other two ministers were cross.

"Why should Daniel be more important than us," they grumbled.

"He's not even from this land," whispered one.

"And he only praises his own god!" whispered the other.

Together, they came up with
a plan to get rid of Daniel.

The two ministers went to see the king. "Oh King, you are so great!" they cried. "Make a law saying that everyone should praise only you for thirty days!"

The king liked to be praised, so he listened to them.

"Whoever breaks the law must then be thrown into the lions' den," they said. The king agreed to make it the law.

For thirty days, everyone
praised the king.

But Daniel went home,
knelt at the window
and praised God,
just as he always did.

The two ministers were
spying on Daniel.

When they saw him
praising God,
they went straight
to the king.

"Oh King, you are so great!" they cried,
"Daniel praised his god. He has broken the law."
When the king heard this he was very sad.

"Whoever breaks the law must then
be thrown into the lions' den," they said.
"The law is the law," sighed the king.

Daniel was taken to the deep, dark den.
Inside, the lions prowled and growled.

Daniel was
lowered down
into the den.

Grrr!

The lions sniffed
and snarled.

The king looked down into the den.
"I hope your God takes care of you,
Daniel," he called sadly.

A big rock was rolled over the den
so that there was no escape.

Daniel sat in the gloomy den.
The lions circled around him.

Then an angel appeared
and the lions settled down.

The king went back to his palace.

He couldn't eat.

He couldn't work.

He couldn't sleep.

All night long, he tossed and turned in his bed.

The next morning, as soon as the sun came up, the king hurried to the lions' den. He gave orders to roll back the stone.

"Daniel!" he called, "has God saved you from the lions?"

"Oh King, you are great!" called Daniel. "God sent an angel to tame the lions. I am safe."

The king was so happy as Daniel was lifted from the den. There wasn't a mark on him anywhere!

The king made a new law.

From that time on, everyone in the land should worship God. "God's law is the law," he said.

Grrr!

# Next Steps

Look back through the book to find more to talk about and join in with.

* Copy the actions. Pretend you are a lion prowling in the den. Bow down and praise the king.

* Join in with the rhyme. Pause to encourage joining in with 'Whoever breaks the law must then/be thrown into the lions' den.'

* Counting pairs. Talk about what a pair means – is it the same as counting in twos? Look back through the book to find pairs.

* Colourful crown. Name the colours in king Saul's crown together, then look back to spot the colours on other pages.

* All shapes and sizes. Compare the two ministers and talk about tall, short, thin, fat.

* Listen to the sounds. When you see the word on the page, point and make the sound – Grrr!

Now that you've read the story... what do you remember?

* Who was Daniel?
* Why was he the king's favourite?
* Why did Daniel pray to God?
* Where did Daniel end up?
* What happened when Daniel was in the lions' den?
* How did Daniel get out of the den?

What does the story tell us?
We don't have to be afraid of scary things because God is looking after us.